Step This Way

A Course for 5-7s in the Church

Book 1

Edited by Marjorie Freeman

Compiled by
Jan Ainsworth, Pamela Egan
Marjorie Freeman, Rosemary Holmes
Barbara Marsh and Tessa Yates

National Society/Church House Publishing
Church House, Great Smith Street, London SW1P 3NZ

THE NATIONAL SOCIETY
A Christian Voice in Education

The National Society (Church of England) for Promoting Religious Education is a charity which supports all those involved in Christian education – teachers and school governors, students and parents, clergy and lay people – with the resources of its RE Centres, archives, courses and conferences.

Founded in 1811, the Society was chiefly responsible for setting up the nationwide network of Church schools in England and Wales and still provides grants for building projects and legal and administrative advice for headteachers and governors. It now publishes a wide range of books, pamphlets and audio-visual items, and two magazines **Crosscurrent** and **Together**.

For details of membership of the Society please contact the Promotions Secretary, The National Society, Church House, Great Smith Street, London SW1P 3NZ.

ISBN 0 7151 4768 4

First published in 1992 by The National Society and Church House Publishing

© The National Society (Church of England) for Promoting Religious Education

Permission is granted for photocopies of the TAKE IT HOME sheets to be made by the purchaser or the purchaser's organisation for use within that organisation only. The remainder of this publication may not be reproduced or transmitted in any form or by any means, electronic or mechanical, including photocopy, or stored in any information, storage and retrieval system, without permission in writing from the publisher.

Illustrations by Terry Jones
Text design by Andrew Haughton, *aj designs*
Cover design by Diane Barker at *The Creative House*

Printed by The Ludo Press Ltd, London SW18 3DG

Contents

Introduction *4*

All About Us

1 Getting to know each other 5
2 Things we can do 8
3 Our favourite things 11

We Gather Round the Table

4 We all need food 14
5 Having a party 17
6 A special meal with Jesus 20
7 Bread 23
8 Wine 26
9 Hands 29

Our Families

10 This is my family 32
11 A day with Jesus' family 35
12 Playing and working together 38
13 Jesus' family prepares for his birth 41
14 Presents for the family 44

Looking at Jesus

15 Following Jesus 47
16 Listening to his stories 50
17 Trusting Jesus 53
18 Jesus helps us to be brave 56
19 Being quiet with Jesus 59
20 Jesus is special 62

Introduction

Christians on the way of faith learn from one another about their beliefs, their ways of living the Christian life and what it means to belong to the Church.

In this book we are providing help for leaders of children's groups, congregations and parents to share their faith with five to seven year olds, to invite them to *Step This Way* on the Christian journey.

GAMES are suggested to introduce each learning session. Use them to get your time together off to a good start.

The TALK AND DO activities are intended to open up conversations with the children about the subject for the day. Encourage the children to talk along the lines suggested both as they work and immediately afterwards.

MORE THINGS TO DO with them are also given so that there will be plenty to keep the young people busy and interested.

Each session contains a STORY to be told. Read the outlines carefully, think about them, see the events in your mind's eye, and share what you see and hear in your imagination with the children.

WORSHIP suggestions are brief so that you can fit them into your normal pattern. There is a Bible reading for which you will need a modern translation, a short prayer, and also one suggestion for a hymn or song which is taken from *Junior Praise* (compiled by Peter Horrobin and Greg Leavers, published by Marshall Pickering) or from *Come and Sing* (compiled by Pamela Dowman and Elspeth M. Stephenson, published by Scripture Union). Choose a song from your own repertoire if you prefer.

Included also are ideas for SHARING WITH ADULTS what the children have done. Please use them whenever possible to give the children an opportunity to get to know the rest of the congregation.

Finally there is a TAKE IT HOME paper each week so that parents can chat with their children about what they have been doing. Permission to photocopy these pages is given free of charge, so make as many copies as you need.

Above all enjoy your time with the children and travel with them on the journey of faith.

All About Us

1 Getting to know each other

A Game

Hold hands in a ring with one person in the middle. Sing 'Round and round and round we go, finding somebody we know.' twice, to the tune of *Twinkle twinkle little star*. The person in the middle points to someone in the circle and says the name. That person goes into the middle. Repeat until everyone has had a turn.

You will need

- ✔ felt pens, large name cards (one each)
- ✔ outline drawings of a child (one each)
- ✔ blu tak or glue
- ✔ large sheet of paper with an outline of your church

Talk and Do

Let the children colour and decorate their name cards. As they do so, talk with them about themselves – their colour of eyes and hair, the clothes they are wearing, the things they like to do, etc. Discover that we are all the same in some ways, but all very different in others. We are all loved by God and we have come together to learn about him.

Story of Mark and Julie's new home

Tell the story, adding your own details, of Mark and Julie who have just moved to a 'new' house in a different area. They miss their old friends and all the children at their new school seem to have friends already. Mum comes home with a job for them – one of the helpers for the sale at their new church needs someone to colour the posters. There are forty posters to be done. 'The sale will be over before we've done them', says Julie. But Mum has a list of the children who belong to the church. We will invite them to a 'colouring picnic' she says.

It rains on the day of the picnic, but they have a treasure hunt for felt pens all over the house, and then colour the posters on the living room floor. One of the girls says she has a dog and asks Julie to go and see him next day. Some of the boys talk about football and Mark arranges to play with them next Saturday. When the posters are finished Mum brings in drinks and food. After their new friends have gone home Mark says, 'I am beginning to like it here!' 'So am I', says Julie. 'I hope we can do something else like that to help at the church', says Mark. 'Like walking dogs?', asks Julie hopefully!

Safety pin sellotaped to back

More things to do

Ask each child to colour in an outline to make a picture of himself or herself. Stick the finished pictures on to the outline of the church. Choose a title and write it on.

Worship

Bible Reading:
Luke 6.12-16 Jesus chooses his twelve helpers.

Prayer:
Dear God, we remember all our friends, especially (mention each child in the group by name). Thank you for helping us to get to know each other. Help us to learn to know you as we meet together each week.

Song:
If I were a butterfly (JP:94)

Sharing with adults

Invite the adults to write their names on badges or on the picture of the church

Take it home

Getting to know each other

Join the dots

> Draw a picture of an adult in your family

> Ask someone to draw a picture of you

Which people in your family look like one another? _____

O God we pray for all the people we love, especially _____ Thank you for their love for us. Help us to remember how much you love us.

Luke 6. 12 to 16

All About Us

2 Things we can do

A Game

Say together, with actions:
Upstairs.....................(stretch up)
Downstairs................(crouch down)
We're busy all day .....(run on spot)
Sometimes we work ..(stand with feet together)
Sometimes we play ....(arms stretched,
                        legs apart)
Like this... ....(one child chooses a
                        mime and everyone
                        copies it e.g. writing,
                        digging, swimming)
Repeat as many times as you like.

You will need
- felt pens
- sheets of thin card, with circles ready drawn, scissors
- cocktail sticks

Talk and Do

Try lots of different activities – hopping, jumping, whistling etc. Talk about the things they like doing and what they are good at doing.

Story of Joe's big voice

'Hey Mum!' shouted Joe. 'Do you know where my football socks are? I've lost them. MUM!' 'Joe, there's no need to shout,' said Mum. 'They're here in the kitchen.' Joe tried to push the socks into his school bag, but the bag was too full. 'Dad, can you help me?' shouted Joe. 'I can't shut my bag.' 'There's no need to shout,' said Dad as he came to help sort the bag out.

Joe was just going out to school when he remembered something important. 'Guess what?' he shouted. 'We're having a class outing on Friday, to a farm.' 'Joe, there's no need to shout,' said his mum and dad together.

When Friday came, everyone in Joe's class was excited. 'My dad says there will be lots of animals to see, 'shouted Joe to his teacher, Mrs Ames. 'There's no need to shout, Joe,' said Mrs Ames.

At the farm there was so much to see that the time passed very quickly. (Elaborate on this) They were just having a last look around when Joe suddenly shouted, 'Look! There's smoke coming out of the barn. Look! Help! The hay must have caught fire. HELP!!' And he shouted again as loudly as he could, 'HELP! FIRE!'

The farmer was a long way away, talking to Mrs Ames, but Joe's shout was so loud that he heard it. He took one look, ran to phone the fire brigade and then rushed to the barn. The fire brigade arrived very quickly. The firemen soon had the blaze under control and stopped it spreading any further.

'It's a good job you have such a loud voice, Joe,' said the farmer. 'I might have lost the other barns and some of the animals as well if you hadn't shouted so quickly and so loudly. Thank you Joe.'

Joe couldn't wait to get home to tell his parents all about it. 'That was one time when it was good to have a loud voice,' said Dad, giving him a hug. 'It was a great day,' shouted Joe. 'Joe, there's no need to shout now!' said his mum and dad together.

More things to do

Let the children cut out the circles from the card. Ask them to draw things they are good at on one side and to write 'Thank you God' on the other. Make a hole in the centre and push a cocktail stick through. Enjoy spinning them.

Worship

Bible reading:
1 Samuel 16.19-23 David plays for Saul when he is unwell.

Prayer:
Thank you God for our eyes to see, our hands to make things, our legs to move, our voices to speak. Thank you for all the things we are good at doing. Thank you for our fun together.

Song:
There are hundreds of sparrows (JP:246)

Sharing with adults

Let the children show some of the things they are good at, and share the prayer with the adults.

Take it home

Things we can do

Colour this picture as well as you can

Draw a picture, or write down, something one of your family is good at doing

1 Samuel 16:19 to 23

We thank you God that we can do so many things well. Help us always to try to do our best, for Jesus' sake Amen.

All About Us

3 Our favourite things

A Game

The leader begins by saying, 'I like, I like, I very much like something beginning with ...' Think of a food for the children to guess. The one who guesses thinks of another one. Repeat with other categories – colours, animals etc.

You will need
- ✔ catalogues, magazines, scissors, glue
- ✔ large sheets of coloured paper, felt pens

Talk and Do

Cut out pictures from catalogues and magazines to make a large composite picture of favourite people and activities. Talk about the children's choice of pictures, and also about favourite activities and people at church or in your group. Add these ideas to the picture, using drawings by the children or writing by the leader.

Story of Miss Jones' class

Some of Miss Jones' class were arguing in the playground. John said, 'She likes me best, because I'm good at Maths.' Susan said, 'She likes me best because I brought her some flowers.' Emily said, 'She likes me best because I carry her bag into school.' James said, 'She likes me best because she says I read very well.' (Add details of other children) Tom was very quiet because he was always in trouble. Before they knew where they were they were all shouting at once, and then started to hit out at one another!

At that moment Miss Jones came to call them in. 'Whatever are you squabbling about?' she asked. There was a sudden silence. Then Emily began to explain, and then they all began to speak at once. Miss Jones said, 'Calm down. Let's all go inside and talk about this quietly.' In the classroom she asked John to tell her all about it. When he had finished she said 'What a silly thing to fight about. I like John because he works well, especially at Maths. I like Susan because she is so cheerful. I like Emily because she always tries to help people. I like James because he is always ready to try new things. (Add others as necessary.) And I like Tom because he does try to keep out of trouble and he makes me laugh. So you see that I like all of you for different reasons.'

Tell your group what you like about each one of them.

More things to do

Look at a large Bible story and picture book together. Talk about some of the pictures and choose one or two stories to read. Decide which picture and which story the children like best.

Worship

Bible reading:
Mark 9.33-37 Who is the greatest?

Prayer:
Thank you, God, for all the things which we enjoy. Thank you for ... (mention some of the activities and people on the large picture) We thank you that each one of us is important to you.

Song:
Things we enjoy (CS:9)

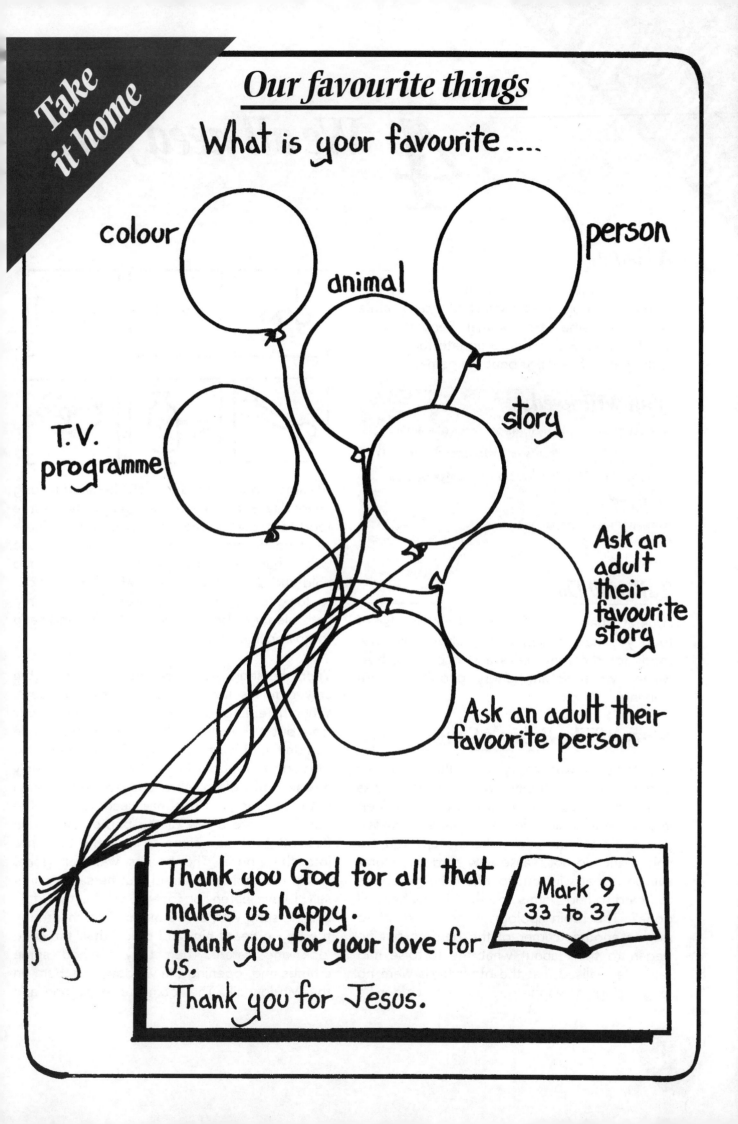

We Gather Round the Table

4 We all need food

A Game

Put cards with pictures or names of foods around the room. Give each child a card with a picture or name of an animal. Send them to find the card with the appropriate food. Look at the pairs of cards. Repeat the game.

> ### You will need
> ✔ a set of cards with pictures or names of animals
> ✔ a matching set of cards with foods for the animals
> ✔ examples of foods e.g. bowl of cornflakes, a cake, a sausage roll
> ✔ large sheet of paper, felt pens

Talk and Do

Look at, share and talk about the examples of food you have brought. Talk about favourite foods for different meals and occasions; how we feel when we are hungry; people who are starving.

Story of The Robin's Song

The tortoise was angry with the robin for singing so cheerfully when winter was approaching. 'Just as I am about to go to sleep in this comfortable hole I have made for myself you begin to sing and wake me up. You are young and do not realise how hard the winter will be. What will you do when the ground is too hard to find worms and the berries have all gone?' The robin apologised and flew off to sing in another corner of the garden, but he began to think about what the tortoise had said. He realised that the other birds were no longer singing. As the days became colder he

became more worried, but still he sang a song every day. Every day he managed to find some food to eat. Then the weather changed. There were heavy snow storms and afterwards there was a hard frost. Everywhere was white and cold and the robin was very afraid. He set out to look for food and discovered a holly tree with plenty of berries. He ate his fill, and sang for joy once more.

Then the snow storms returned and the robin stayed in his ivy covered hole for two days. When he emerged he went straight to the holly tree, but it seemed smaller than before, and he couldn't find a single berry. He was very anxious and flew about in great distress. Suddenly he saw a pile of holly branches which had been cut ready for the Christmas decorations in the house. He ate a few of the berries, and then flew off as a man came to take the branches into the house. The berries were all gone! Again the robin was afraid, but he said to himself 'I have eaten for today. I will be thankful,' and he sang with all his might. The children in the house heard him and called their father to look and listen. Then they fetched some crumbs and, opening the window, put them on the window sill. The robin ate every one and

then he sang again. Every day, after that, until the weather began to get warmer the children put out food for the robin, and always he sang his thanks after he had eaten. Once he was sure that spring had really come, the robin sang loudly by the tortoise's winter home and woke him from his rest. 'I have eaten every day,' he told him, 'and sung my song of thanks.'
(Adapted from 'Daily Bread' in *Parables from Nature* by Mrs Gatty)

More things to do

Make up a prayer or song of thanks for food. Include examples of food which the children especially enjoy, and remember those who are hungry. Write it up on a large sheet of paper and let the children decorate it with their drawings of food.

Worship

Bible reading:
John 6.1-11. Jesus feeds 5,000 people

Prayer:
For all our food, we thank you God
For all those who prepare it for us, we thank you God
For all your many gifts to us, we thank you God.

Song:
A boy gave to Jesus (JP:1)

Sharing with adults

Show them the prayer or song and invite them to say or sing it with the children.

Take it home

We all need food

Which animals like these foods?

Milk — Apple — Cheese
Banana — Bone

Cat   Dog   Mouse   Horse   Monkey

Draw your favourite meal on this plate

Ask an adult to tell you their favourite meal. Draw it on this plate.

John 6
1 to 11

Thank you Father for our food.
Thank you Lord for all things good.

We Gather Around the Table

5 Having a party

A Game

The children make a circle and walk around singing to the tune of Mulberry Bush or Nuts in May: 'Who shall we ask to hoover the floor, hoover the floor, hoover the floor? Who shall we ask to hoover the floor, so we can have a party?'

Choose one child to do the action while the rest sing, '(John) is going to hoover the floor ... so we can have a party.'
Repeat with other actions e.g. set the table, make the cakes wrap the presents.

You will need
✔ paper plates, magazines and scissors or Play-Doh
✔ table cloth, serviettes, paper plates, paper cups,
✔ felt pens or gummed shapes
✔ orange juice, biscuits, flowers, a vase

Talk and Do

Give each child a paper plate Ask them to cut out pictures of food from magazines or make models of food, to put on the plates for a party, Talk about food that is especially nice at parties, games they play at parties, different kinds of parties that they have been to.

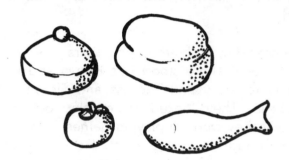

Story of Wayne's Party

Wayne's mum had said that Wayne could have a party. Wayne hadn't many friends but he thought it would be fun to have a party. He thought about the children at school. 'I will invite Sophie Swankalot and Brian Bigspender and Ivor Lotacash.' So he said to his mother 'There will be three people coming to my party.'

The next day at school he told Sophie and Brian and Ivor, 'I'm going to have a birthday party next Saturday. It's at three o'clock. We shall have some good games and lots of food. I want you three to come.' Simon and Brian and Ivor seemed pleased to be asked.

On Friday Wayne reminded them about the party. Sophie said, 'Oh dear. We are all going ice skating tomorrow, I can't come.' Brian said, 'My Dad's promised to buy me a new bike and I'm going to choose it. I can't come.' Ivor said, 'Dad's promised to take me to the football match, in the directors' seats. I won't be coming after all.'

As soon as he got home his mother said, 'What's the matter? Can't they come?' 'No,' said Wayne, 'None of them are coming, so I can't have a party.' His mother looked at all the food she had been getting ready. She looked at Wayne's unhappy face. 'Well, someone will have to eat all this food,' she said. 'I've got an idea. Mrs Brown is looking after some foster children. Their parents can't have them at home at the moment. They won't have any friends around here. Let's give her a ring and see if they would like to come.' Wayne wasn't very keen at first, but his mum rang Mrs Brown and explained what had happened. Mrs Brown said, 'I'll just go and ask them.' In a little while she was back. 'They would love to come,' she said.

The next day, at three o'clock, there was a ring at the bell. There stood Mrs Brown and with her were Tracy and Thomas and Simon and Michelle. They looked rather shy, but very quickly they were all playing games. They had each brought him a present. He got a new biro, some sellotape, a packet of sweets and some transfer pictures. They all had a lovely time. They played lots of good games and had a stupendous tea. Wayne's mum lit the candles on his birthday cake. He wished and blew them out and they all sang 'Happy Birthday'.

At last it was time for them to go home. 'Thank you for asking us to your party. You must come and see us soon.' 'I'm glad you came,' said Wayne, 'it was the best party ever!'

More things to do

Share some juice and biscuits together, making it a party occasion. With the children's help lay the table with a pretty cloth and serviettes. Decorate paper plates and beakers with felt pens or gummed shapes. Arrange some flowers. Say or sing a grace before the 'meal'. Play a favourite game afterwards.

Worship

Bible reading:
Luke 14.16-24 The story of the great feast

Prayer:
Thank you, God, for food and games. Thank you, God, for parties and fun.

Song:
Thank you Lord (JP:232)

Sharing with adults

Show the adults the plates with pictures or models of party foods. Sing or say grace with them.

Take it home

Having a party

Find the food hidden in this picture

When is the next party in your family?

- -

Thank you for party times when we remember special occasions in our families and in our lives. Help us to make every mealtime and every day a special day when we remember your love.

Luke 14 16 to 24

We Gather Round the Table

6 A special meal with Jesus

A Game

Fasten some bread rolls on pieces of string and hold them or tie them up. Let each child try to take a bite.

> ### You will need
> ✔ soft bread rolls, string
> ✔ a tablecloth, chalice, paten, bottle or cruet of wine, water, wafers or bread.
> ✔ paper, felt pens

Talk and Do

Let the children look at the communion things and help you to set them out on the table. You might let them taste the wafers or bread and the wine. Talk about the communion service in your own church – what happens, how the things are used. Encourage the children to tell you what they know, and add to their information as necessary.

Story of The Last Supper

On the night before Jesus died he had a very special meal with his disciples. He sent two of them to get the room ready. 'Go secretly so that no-one knows where we are,' he said. 'It is very dangerous for us here in Jerusalem at this time.' Two of them went ahead to get things ready and the rest made their way in twos and threes, quietly and secretly, to the upstairs room where they were to meet.

During the meal Jesus took a piece of bread. He said a prayer and asked God to bless it, and then he broke it in pieces and he gave each of them a part. 'Take, eat this,' he said. 'Whenever you eat bread like this, remember me.' Then he took a cup of wine. He thanked God for it and then he said, 'All of you, drink this to remember me by. This is my life which I am giving to you.' So each one took a drink of wine and thought about his words. They didn't understand, but they knew that this was a very special meal.

Later that night Jesus was arrested by the soldiers and the next day he was killed on the cross. Then the disciples began to understand what Jesus had been talking about. He had given his life for them. They knew that they would always remember him.

More things to do

Ask the children to draw pictures, either of the communion service in church, or of the last supper. Write under all the pictures 'Do this to remember me.'

Sharing with adults

Show them the pictures and say the prayer together.

Worship

Bible reading:
1 Corinthians 11.23-25 The last supper

Prayer:
O God, we remember how Jesus shared the last supper with his friends before he died on the cross. We remember him and his love for us as we think about that story and we thank you for all that he does for us.

Song:
Jesus is a friend of mine (JP:136)

Take it home

A special meal with Jesus

Put a ring around the things we use in the communion service, and colour them in.

Think of one thing to remind you about each person in your family

Jesus we remember that you lived, died and rose again.
We remember that you are with us now.
We are glad and we praise you

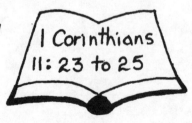

1 Corinthians 11: 23 to 25

We Gather Round the Table

7 Bread

A Game

The leader begins by saying, 'I went out to tea and I had bread and jam.' One of the children continues, 'I went out to tea and I had bread and jam, and a piece of toast.' The children take it in turns to go through the sentence, each adding an item which includes bread. Go on to other kinds of food when ideas about bread run out. Those who cannot remember the items 'lose a life' or drop out.

Talk and Do

Make a collage of pictures of bread of different kinds, and its ingredients. Talk about the meals at which the children eat bread, how it is made, making flour etc.

You will need

✔ large sheet of paper or card, magazine pictures of breads, empty packets of flour, dried yeast, sugar, salt
✔ scissors, glue
✔ ingredients to make sandwiches, serviettes

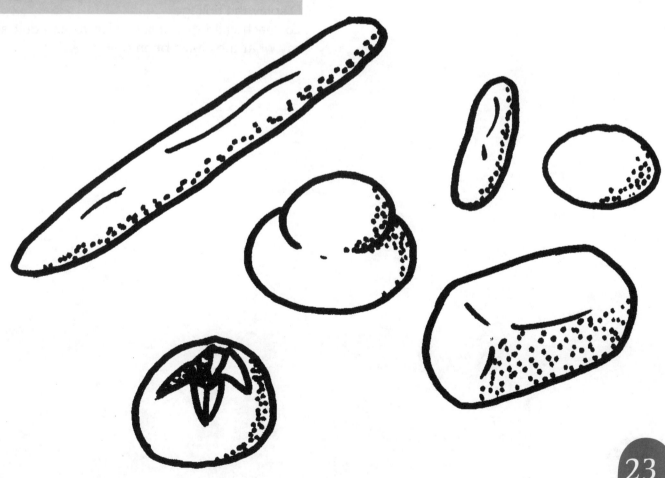

Story of a Loaf of Bread

The baker had been busy making bread, mixing the yeast with sugar and water, then mixing it into the flour and salt, letting it rise, then forming it into loaves, leaving them to rise again, and then putting them into the oven to bake. When the loaves were golden brown the baker took them out of the oven and put them to cool. Then he put them on the shelf in his shop ready to sell them.

At the end of the afternoon there was only one loaf left, and that was one which had become rather squashed at the bottom of the shelf. 'No-one will want this loaf,' said the baker. Just at that moment a young man came into the shop. 'Oh please have you any bread left?' he said. I've just got back from holiday and I have nothing in the house to eat, except a bit of butter and some cheese.' He was glad to buy the squashed loaf. He had it for tea with some cheese, he made some toast for breakfast, he had bread and cheese for lunch, and he gave the last bits to the birds, so nothing was wasted.

More things to do

Look at some communion wafers or bread. Remember again the story of the last supper. Let the children help to make some small sandwiches, enough for them to have two each
Say a grace and let them eat their own sandwiches. Wrap the other sandwiches in serviettes.

Worship

Bible reading:
1 Kings 17.1-6 The ravens feed Elijah

Prayer:
O God, we remember Jesus at his last meal with his friends. We remember how he took the bread and shared it . We remember that he died for us and we thank you for Jesus

Song:
God takes good care of me (SG:14)

Sharing with adults

Display the collage.
Let each child give a sandwich to an adult and say what they have been doing.

Take it home

Bread

Put numbers by these pictures to show the story of bread

○ the seed grows
○ baking bread
○ grinding corn
○ sowing seed
○ cutting corn
○ sharing bread

Find out how many loaves of bread your family eats each week

Thank you God for bread
Thank you for Jesus
Thank you for life

1 Kings 17
1 to 6

We Gather Round the Table

8 Wine

A Game

Blindfold each child in turn and give him or her a sip of a drink to guess what it is. If any of the children are unhappy about being blindfolded let them close their eyes instead.

You will need

- ✔ a variety of drinks in small beakers e.g. orange juice, milk, lemon juice, water
- ✔ grapes, spoons, saucer, glasses, serviettes, a bottle of grape juice
- ✔ egg boxes, brass paper-fasteners, kitchen foil, gummed shapes or sequins, scissors, glue

Talk and do

Let the children take turns to crush the grapes onto a saucer with a spoon, Pour the juice into a glass. If there is enough give everyone a taste, or use some bottled grape juice. Talk about making wine, special drinks for parties, drinking a toast. Pretend to drink toasts for a birthday, a baptism, a wedding etc., the leader making the intoductory 'speech' and the children pretending to drink. Let the children make the speeches if they wish. Pour out some grape juice for everyone and propose a toast to Jesus, using the children's ideas about what to say.

Story of a bottle of wine

Emma and William were going with their Mum to a very special party. Nan and Grandad had been married for fifty years, so it was their Golden Wedding party. All the aunts and uncles and cousins were going and Mum had been very busy making a special cake. (Let the children suggest how the cake would be decorated, and what there would be to eat.) Emma and William had made a card. (What would be on it?) They had bought presents, a yellow scarf for Nan and a yellow tie for Grandad.

In the cupboard William found a bottle of wine. 'Where did this come from?' he asked. 'I bought it last Christmas,' said Mum. 'But where did you get it?' 'From the supermarket' said Mum. 'But where did they get it?' 'From the wine merchants I expect.' 'But where did they get it?' 'From the vineyards, where the grapes were grown in the sunshine and then picked and crushed and bottled and left until the wine was ready to drink.' 'Oh I see,' said William. 'Can we take it with us,' he said, 'to drink their health?' 'There will be plenty of wine there,' said Mum 'and some juice for you children.'

On the day of the party the children put on their best clothes. William put their presents in a big bag. Mum thought it was rather a large bag, but she didn't say so, and she didn't know that at the bottom of it was the bottle of wine!

The party was great. The cousins played together, the adults talked and talked, and the food was very good. At last it was time for the toasts. 'Can we have some real wine?' said William and Emma. 'I don't think there is any. It's just been poured into everyone's glasses for the toast.' said Mum. 'I've got some!' said William, and he reached into his big bag under his chair, and pulled out his bottle of wine. Everyone began to laugh and Uncle David opened the bottle and all the children had a little drop in their glasses to drink the toast. 'What a good thing I brought it!' said William, and proudly stood up to drink a toast to 'Nan and Grandad'.

More things to do

Let each child make a model chalice. Cut the 'cups' from the egg boxes and trim them as shown. Fasten two together with a paper fastener. Cover with foil and decorate them.

Sharing with adults

Drink a toast to Jesus with them.

Worship

Bible reading:
John 2.1-10 Jesus at a wedding

Prayer:
Jesus took the bread and the wine, and shared them with his disciples. He said 'Take this to remember me. This is my life.' Jesus, we remember you, and we are glad that you are alive and close to us now, loving and helping us, although we cannot see you.

Song:
Jesus the best friend (SG:37)

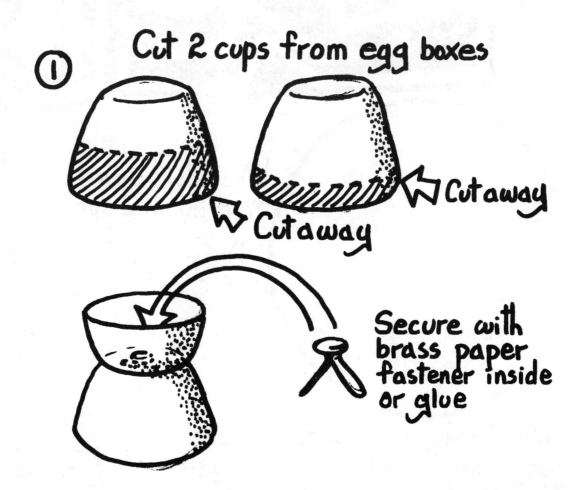

Take it home

Wine

Find the way from the grapes to the bottle.

What does your family like to drink at a special party?

Draw a picture of it.

We thank you, God, for all our happy times together. We pray for all those who are sad today, and ask you to show us ways of helping them

John 2
1 to 10

We Gather Round the Table

9 Hands

A Game

The leader mimes an action using hands (e.g. washing hands, sawing wood, driving a car) for the children to guess. The child who guesses correctly mimes an action for the rest to guess. Repeat until all those who wish have had at least one turn. Repeat the game, this time showing actions in which hands are used in church e.g. praying, baptising, receiving communion.

You will need

✔ coloured paper, scissors, large sheet of paper or card, glue.

Talk and do

Help each child to draw around his or her hand on coloured paper. Write the children's names on their hand shapes and cut them out. Arrange the hand shapes on the large sheet of paper or card in different ways, e.g. to make a circle of hands; in pairs as though offering a gift. Glue them in position. Talk about the many things for which hands are used, some bad and some good. Talk about, and try, shaking hands, and also exchanging the peace in church.

Story of Blessing the Children

Tell the story of Jesus blessing the children (Mark 10.13-16). Emphasise the way in which the disciples and Jesus used their hands. 'The disciples ushered them away from Jesus.' 'Jesus drew them close to him.' 'He lifted the little ones onto his knee.' 'He placed his hands on each one of them.' Finish with, 'For the rest of their lives the children remembered his kind, loving face, the words he said and the feel of his hands upon their heads.'

More things to do

Make up a song about using hands at home and in church. Use an easy tune and plenty of repetition in the words e.g.

'Wash, wash, wash our hands, wash them nice and clean.
   Busily, busily, busily, busily, using hands at home.

Share, share, share the peace, share with everyone.
   Joyfully, joyfully, joyfully, joyfully, using hands in church.'

to the tune of *Row, row, row, row the boat*. It would be good to think of verses connected with food in the home, (e.g. mixing, chopping), and to include actions from the communion service (e.g. blessing, taking).

Worship

Bible reading:
Mark. 10.13-16 Jesus uses his hands to heal the deaf and dumb man

Prayer:
God, we thank you for Jesus, for the kind things he did, for the way he welcomed and blessed the children. Help us to use our hands in kind and loving ways.

Song:
Jesus hands were kind hands. (SG:45, JP:134)

Sharing with adults

Teach the adults the song which the children have made up.

Our Families

10 This is my family

A Game

Put out boxes labelled Mum, Dad, Grandad etc. Hide cut out pictures of people around the room. Let the children search and find them and in turn decide which box they should be put into.

You will need

- ✔ cut out pictures of people of different ages from magazines or catalogues
- ✔ boxes labelled Mum, Dad, Grandma, Grandad, uncles, aunts, babies
- ✔ glue, sheets of paper
- ✔ paper, felt pens
- ✔ small present(s) for adults e.g. a flower, a bar of chocolate

Talk and do

Let each child choose pictures from the boxes so that he or she can stick them on to a sheet of paper to make a picture of his or her own family. Talk about their families, the things which they do for one another etc. Be careful to accept what the children say about their families and ask no insensitive questions.

Story of Nan coming to stay

Build a story around this outline:

Nan is unwell. Mum tells Melanie and Robin and they decide to ask her to live with them. The children are anxious about having to change things around, share a bedroom, move their toys etc.

Preparations: shifting furniture, cleaning the bedroom for Nan, putting her special things around the house, selling Nan's house. Moving day: hard work and chaos. Nan very sad.

First meal together: problems, Nan wants different food, weaker tea, grumbles at the children. Mum explains that Nan is frightened and unhappy after her illness and asks them to be patient.

Next day: just as bad. Arguments about television programmes, doing jobs, running around for Nan, leaving her alone all day. By bedtime everyone is upset and cross. The week passes and gradually everyone begins to get used to one another. Nan beginning to be able to do more.

Friday: Mum and the children come home to wonderful smell of cooking. Nan has made a special meal for a surprise. During the meal they share their news of the day, and plan a birthday party for Melanie. They realise that they have become a family again. Everybody has changed a bit and helped a bit and it will work out quite well.

More things to do

The leader quickly draws a matchstick picture about an event in his or her own family – something that happened in childhood perhaps. Tell the children this story. Let the children draw pictures about something that happened in their families, the best thing they did, the funniest thing, when Dad was a child, when Grandma was little etc. Encourage the children to share and talk about their pictures. Be prepared for sad stories too ('when Dad left us') and accept them with love and reassurance for the child.

Talk about people who live alone. How can the children help them?

Worship

Bible reading:
Luke 2.4-7, 39-40 Mary, Joseph and Jesus

Prayer:
We thank you, God, for our families, and for all who love and care for us. Help us to live together happily, to share with one another, and to help each other. For Jesus' sake.

Song:
Be kind (SG:48)

Sharing with adults

Give a small present to one or more adults in the congregation who live alone. Tell them what you have been doing.

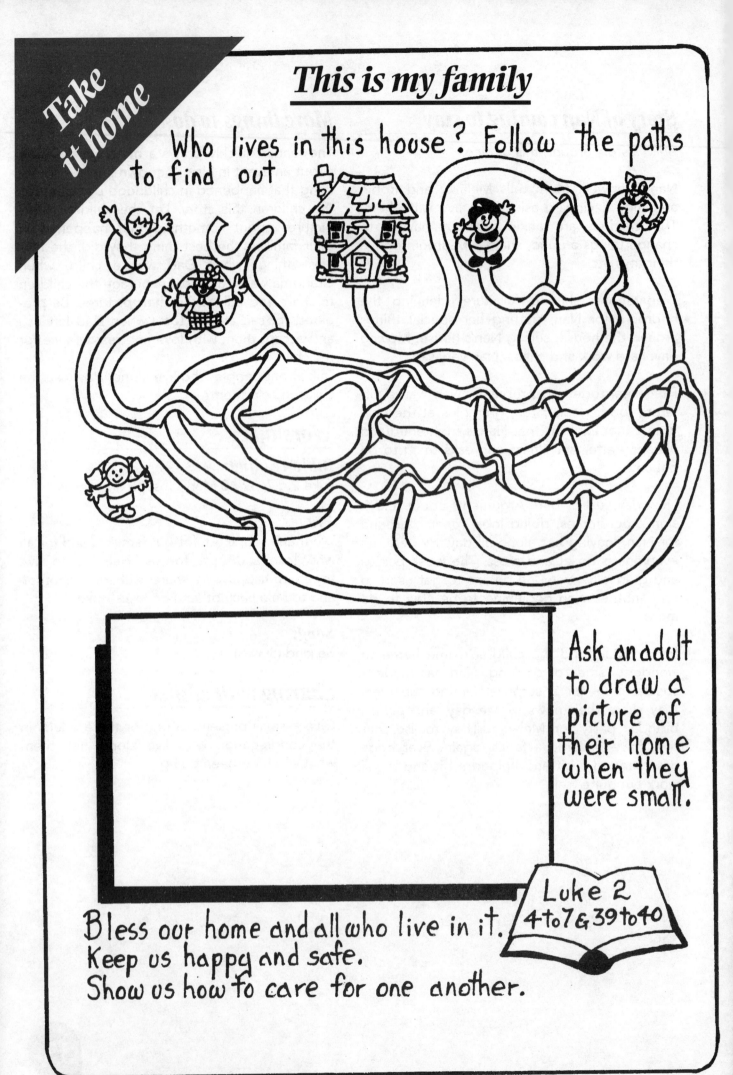

Our Families

11 A day with Jesus' family

A Game

All the children except one sit on a chair. The child without a chair walks amongst them repeating 'Can I come to your house?' At some point he or she says, 'We all move house.' Immediately all the children must move to another chair while he or she tries to sit on a vacant chair. Whoever is left without a chair continues as the 'homeless' one.

You will need
- boxes, paper, felt pens, glue
- Play-Doh, scraps of material, scissors

Talk and do

Use boxes to make models of houses like that in which Jesus lived. Cover the boxes with paper if necessary and mark in the windows, doors, steps. Talk about the differences between Jesus' home and the children's homes, the things they take for granted like water from taps, electricity, gas, television, which did not exist in Jesus' day. How did people manage then?

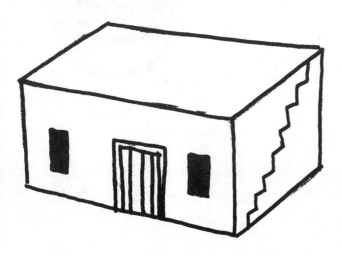

Story of a day in Jesus' home

Tell the story and let the children act it out as you tell it.

When Jesus was a boy his day would be quite different from ours. Let's pretend that we lived in his house. We would sleep on a mattress on the floor. (Lie down on your mattresses.) When it gets light it's time to get up. (Stretch and yawn and get up.) The boys will have to help Joseph to clear out the donkey's dirty straw and put down some fresh straw and feed him. (Off you go, boys.) The girls will help to roll up the mattresses and blankets and put them away. (Off you go, girls.) Now it's time for breakfast. First we wash our hands. (One person pours water from a big jug over the hands of the others.) Now we say our prayers. Say after me "Thank you God for keeping us safe through the night ... Amen." Now we eat our bread and our currants.

It's time for school, but only for the boys. You walk up the hill to the synagogue and sit down. (Boys walk, and sit on the floor.) You will write your letters in the sand on the floor. (Write your name.) The girls have work to do. You will sweep the house with a broom, (the girls sweep) fetch water from the well, (walk to the well with the jugs on their heads, let down the bucket, fill the jugs, walk home) make a fire and do the cooking (fetch sticks, build fire, put food in pot over fire). The boys come home from school (walk home) and play with their friends (play games).

At last it's time for the evening meal. Wash your hands ... sit down ... and use a piece of bread to scoop up some stew from the big bowl in the middle ...

35

Now it's time for prayers again. We go up the steps outside to the roof ... and sit there quietly ... Perhaps Joseph tells a story from the Bible. Then we say "Thank you God for all the blessings of this day ... Amen." It's getting dark. We go down the steps. Mary has put down the mattresses. We lie down and go to sleep. Goodnight. Shalom. Peace.'

More things to do

Use Play-Doh to model some of the things which would have been used in Jesus' family – jugs, lamps, bowls – and make donkeys and people too if time. Make mattresses from pieces of material.

Sharing with adults

Show them the models and talk to them about them.

Worship

Bible reading:
Luke 2. 51-52 Jesus at home in Nazareth

Prayer:
We thank God for Jesus' family:
For Mary and Joseph and his brothers and sisters
For the years they spent looking after him
For the things he learned in his family about caring for one another and helping each other.
Help us to learn to care for each other and to help each other.

Song:
Jesus was born in Bethlehem (SG:25)

Take it home

A day with Jesus family

Draw lines to match these pictures

Our homes **Jesus' home**

Draw a picture of Jesus at school.

Tell an adult about it

Thank you, God,
for all things which help us to be comfortable and happy in our homes.
Show us how to make other people happy

Luke 2
51 to 52

Our Families

12 Playing and working together

A Game

Whisper the name of an object which is used in the home to one child. The child draws the object on a piece of paper for the rest to guess. Whoever guesses correctly is told the next object to draw. Be ready to assist children where necessary.

You will need
- list of everday objects which are used in the family e.g. saucepan, trowel, mug, door key, car
- felt pens, paper

Talk and do

Ask the children to think of other things which are used at home, for cooking, cleaning, gardening, games etc. All mime what the objects are used for. Talk about the things which they do separately and the things they do with other members of the family, activities which are work and those which are for fun.

Story of Jesus' visit to Jerusalem

Tell the story of Jesus going to Jerusalem for the Passover feast when he was twelve years old (Luke 2.41 – 50). Tell them about the journey there, camping out for three nights, doing chores, playing with the other boys, talking with people. Once there they would find a place to hold their special Passover meal, they would visit the great Temple church where animals were sold, where people met to pray and to talk. Describe Mary and Joseph's worry on the way home when they could not find Jesus, their search among the other travellers and friends, their return to Jerusalem and discovery of him in the Temple courtyard talking with the teachers there. He was not playing, but learning about God and preparing for the work he would have to do when he was older.

More things to do

Together make up a story about a family. Decide on the people and their names, and how they will spend one Sunday. Include, for example, going to church, some jobs to be done, an outing. Act out the story.

Worship

Bible reading:
Luke 2.41-50 Jesus is lost

Prayer:
We thank you, God, for all the things we do together in our families. Thank you for times when we ... (list activities drawn and discussed by the children). Thank you for the things we do together in church. Help those who have no families and help us to remember to help them.

Song:
Hands to work (SG:47)

Sharing with adults

Share the pictures of objects, or the acted story, with the congregation.

Take it home

Playing and working together

Colour the things which your family does together.

Draw your own picture of your family

Lord Jesus, we are glad that Mary and Joseph looked after you when you were small. We are glad that we have people to look after us too. Thank you for all the good things of our lives.

Luke 2 41 to 50

Our Families

13 Jesus' family prepares for his birth

A Game

Divide the children into teams of about six and line them up. Put a box of baby things in front of each team. When you call out the name of an item which is needed for a baby, the first child in each team goes to the team's box and finds the item and then runs to the back of the team with it. Repeat with the next children in the lines – until all the items have been fetched.

You will need
- ✔ a box for each team with identical items for a baby in each box e.g. bottle, nappy, shawl, dummy.
- ✔ papers, felt pens or catalogues of baby things and scissors, paste.
- ✔ pieces of strong paper approx. 30cm by 20cm, pieces 15cm by 20cm, sellotape, scissors, scraps of material or coloured paper

Talk and Do

Look at the items from the game and talk about all the things which a baby needs. Let the children draw or cut out pictures of things which would be needed. Talk about the things which cannot be drawn so easily like love and care and our prayers.

Story of Mary and Joseph preparing for Jesus

The children will be looking forward to Christmas, so today tell them the story of the angel's message to Mary (Luke 1.26-31). Joseph too was told about the coming baby. He and Mary were married, and began to prepare for the baby. Let the children help you to decide what they would do. What would Mary and her mother Anne make and do? What would Joseph, a carpenter, do? What plans and arrangements would they make? Tell of the order for everyone to go back to their 'home' town. Joseph would be dismayed when he realised that they would have to go to Bethlehem, a long journey, when the baby's birth was so close. He arranged to take a donkey for Mary to ride. Think of the preparations, packing the food, the baby things etc. What things might have to be left behind? At last they were ready. They said good-bye to their friends and to Anne and set off on their long journey.

More things to do

Begin to make a model of the nativity. Let each child make the figure of Mary and, if time, of Joseph. Give each child one piece of paper of each size and help them to fold them in two and in two again. Push the smaller strip into the larger one and sellotape in place. Draw on a face and make clothes from the scraps of material.

Worship

Bible reading:
Luke 2.1-6 Mary and Joseph go to Bethlehem

Prayer:
As Mary and Joseph prepared for the birth of Jesus they knew that he was God's son. We are glad that he was born into the world to teach about God and to show us how to live. Help us to love him and learn more and more about him.

Song:
Jesus, baby Jesus (SG:18)

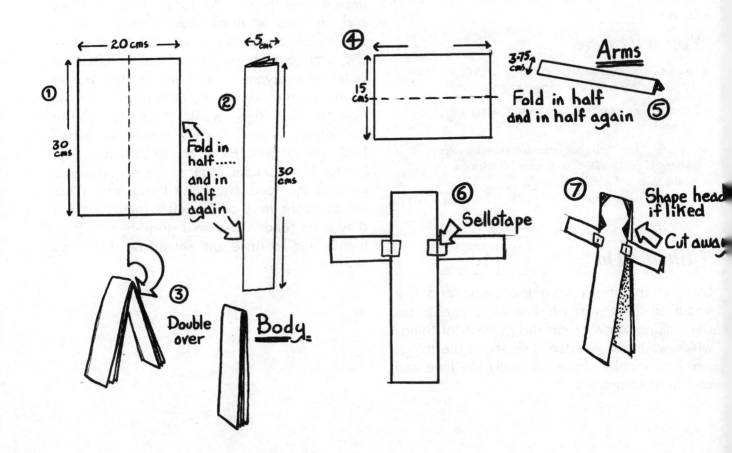

Take it home

Jesus family prepares for his birth

Colour this picture of Mary and Joseph. You could use it for a Christmas card.

O God, help us to prepare ourselves for the birthday of Jesus, so that in all the business we may remember him and his love for us.

Luke 2 1 to 6

Our Families

14 Presents for the family

A Game

Label 'corners' of the room MOTHER, BABY, GRANDFATHER, FRIEND. Call out the name of a present. The children run to the appropriate corner. Be prepared to accept some unexpected decisions – a cookery book might be the right present for Grandfather!

You will need

- ✔ labels – mother, baby, grandfather, friend
- ✔ paper, scissors and glue to make baskets, sweets or nuts
- ✔ icing sugar, egg white, double cream, peppermint essence, colouring, rolling pin, cutters, trays to make peppermint creams
- ✔ coloured postcards or greeting cards, scissors, envelopes, felt pens to make jigsaws
- ✔ strong white paper, coloured paper, glue, spring clothes peg, strong glue to make butterfly decorations
- ✔ Play-Doh

Talk and Do

Let each child make a present to give to a member of his or her family.

e.g. *Paper basket:* fold the paper as shown, cut the solid lines, bend end flaps in and glue, glue or staple the handle. Fill with sweets or nuts.

Peppermint creams: mix together 1 lb icing sugar, white of egg, a little double cream, a few drops of peppermint essence, colouring if required, to make a firm paste. Sprinkle a board with icing sugar and roll out. Cut out shapes, and leave to dry.

Jigsaw: cut up a postcard or colourful greetings card into about 12 pieces. Put the pieces into an envelope and write a title on the outside.

Butterfly decoration: cut out the butterfly shape in strong white paper, and 2 or more different coloured papers. Glue them together down the centre of each butterfly, white at the bottom then each colour in turn. Stick it onto a

clothes peg with strong glue.

Talk about presents which the children will be giving at Christmas, the pleasure of giving as well as of receiving.

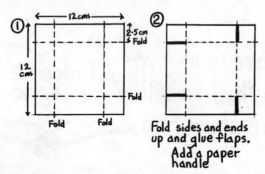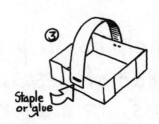

Story of Jesus' birth

Tell the story of Mary and Joseph going to Bethlehem, arriving to find it crowded, and finding nowhere to stay. At last they are offered a stable cave with the animals, and accept it gratefully. There Jesus is born and laid in the feeding trough of the animals. Continue with the story of the angels' message to the shepherds and their visit to the baby. Ask the children about the presents which the shepherds might take to welcome the baby on his birth day.

More things to do

Finish the models of the nativity. Let each child make a manger and a baby from Play-Doh to take home.

Learn a song to sing about Jesus' birthday e.g. Christmas greetings, Christmas joy (SG:52), or make up your own song e.g. 'Mary went up to Bethlehem ... when it was Jesus' birthday' to the tune of The Mulberry Bush.

Worship

Bible reading:
Luke 2.6-16 The shepherds visit the baby

Prayer:
O Jesus, our Saviour, we are glad that you came as a little child to live on earth. Help us to make your birthday a happy day for everyone we love.

Song:
Wonderful Christmas gift (SG:21)

Sharing with adults

Sing the new song as a Christmas present to the congregation and invite them to sing it too.

Take it home

Presents for the family

Find the presents hidden in this picture

Find a box and make it into a stable for your models of Mary, Joseph and Jesus

O come let us adore him
O come let us adore him
O come let us adore him
Christ the Lord

Luke 2
6 to 16

Looking at Jesus

15 Following Jesus

A Game

Play follow my leader. Begin with an adult leading the children, then allow some of the children to lead if they wish. Finish with an adult so that the children end by sitting down ready for the next activity.

You will need

- ✔ cut out figures of disciples, felt pens, large sheet of paper, glue.
- ✔ cards to make invitations

Talk and Do

Let each child colour in a prepared cut out picture of a disciple, while the leader colours in a figure to represent Jesus. Arrange the figures in different ways on the large sheet of paper - in a circle, in a line etc. Discuss what they are doing in each case. Decide which arrangement to keep and glue the figures in place. Talk about the names of the disciples and the things that they did with Jesus. Draw out from them that 'following him' meant being with him, learning from him and trying to be like him – things which we can try to do also.

Story of Matthew's call

Tell the story of Matthew's call (Matthew 9.9-12). Matthew collected money for the Romans who had taken over the country. He had to charge people more than the proper taxes so that he had some money to live on because he was not paid any wages for doing so. No one liked the tax collectors because of this, and so Matthew must have been very surprised and happy when Jesus told him to give it all up and be one of his followers. He gave a great party for Jesus and asked all his old friends, tax collectors and other unpopular folk. Some people were very surprised and asked, 'Why does Jesus share a meal with people like this?' Jesus heard them and said, 'It is people like this who specially need me.' Matthew must have been very glad to hear him say so, and very proud when, later on, Jesus chose him for one of his special disciples.

More things to do

Ask the children about the first time they came to church or to the group. Who brought them? Is there anyone they could ask to come with them? Let each child make an invitation to give to a friend, or to ask members of the congregation to come and see what their group does. Help them to write in the name and then let them decorate it with pictures of things they use in the group – pens, books, musical instruments etc.

Worship

Bible reading:
Matthew 9.9-12 Jesus calls Matthew

Prayer:
Help us to learn about Jesus, to talk with him in our prayers and to do the things which would please him.

Song:
Jesus I will come with you (JP:138)

Sharing with adults

Show the picture and tell them about it. Give out the invitations.

Take it home

Following Jesus

Here are some ways of learning about Jesus. Colour in the ones you like best.

Draw a picture of someone you like to do things with

Jesus, may we know you more clearly,
love you more dearly, and
follow you more nearly,
day by day

Matthew 9 9 to 12

Looking at Jesus

16 Listening to his stories

A Game

Play 'I spy'. If your children are very young use colours or categories instead of initial letters e.g. 'I spy with my little eye something that is pink' or 'something that I can play with.'

You will need

- ✓ 3 or 4 bags with three objects in each e.g. a ball, a biscuit, a beaker.
- ✓ paper, felt pens

Talk and Do

Take the objects out of one of the bags, and make up a simple story about it. e.g. Amy had a new ball. She played in the garden with it but put it down while she had a beaker of orange. A dog ran off with the ball. Amy called him, gave him a biscuit and he dropped the ball. She finished her drink and played with her ball.

Take the objects from another bag and encourage the children to help you to tell a story about them. Repeat until all the bags are used. Talk about stories they enjoy hearing, reading, watching on television, hearing about Jesus.

Story of the sower

Tell the story of the sower (Matthew 13.1-8). First set the scene – Jesus sitting in the boat, able to see the crowds and over their heads to the countryside, watching a sower going up and down a field throwing seed from his basket, first to the right and then to the left. He draws people's attention to the sower and then tells the story of the seed falling on different kinds of soil. Let the parable stand alone without any explanation of its meaning, except to conclude by saying, 'Some of the crowd listening knew that Jesus was talking about the way they listened to, and followed, God's word. Some remembered and acted on it, and some forgot all about it.'

More things to do

Tell one or two more short stories told by Jesus. The seed growing secretly (Mark 4.26-29) or the lost coin (Luke 15.8-9) would be suitable. Let the children draw them or act them out.

Sharing with adults

Ask some adults which of the stories which Jesus told they like best.

Worship

Bible reading:
Matthew 13.1-8 The story of the sower

Prayer:
Thank you, God, for the stories which we enjoy. Thank you for the stories which Jesus told and which we can hear today.

Song:
Tell me the stories of Jesus (verse 1) (JP:228)

Take it home

Listening to his stories

Look at these pictures about a story Jesus told. Colour them in

Ask someone to help you find the story in Luke 15:4-6

Jesus, help us to listen and to understand and so to know more about you and about our world.

Matthew 13 1 to 3

Looking at Jesus

17 Trusting Jesus

A Game

Set out an obstacle course with chairs etc. Blindfold one of the children and let an adult lead them around the course. Let other children have a turn and allow some of the children to be guides if they wish.

You will need

- ✔ blindfold
- ✔ bandaged doll or teddy, spoons, empty medicine bottles
- ✔ cards, felt pens, coloured paper, scissors, glue

Talk and Do

Discuss what is wrong with the doll or teddy. Let the children pretend to help him. Think of other illnesses and injuries and let the children pretend to treat these also. Talk about times when they have been unwell, ill, have hurt themselves. Who looks after them? Who do they like to be there when things go wrong or they are ill?

Story of a man who trusted Jesus

Tell the story of the healing of the officer's servant (Matthew 8.5-13). Tell the story from the point of view of the Roman officer who had heard of Jesus and his powers: 'I am sure that he will be able to make my servant better. I will go and ask him.' Show his unwillingness to put Jesus to unnecessary trouble: 'You need not come to the house, just say the word and he will be healed.' He hears Jesus say, 'I have never found anyone here with such great faith. Go home. Your servant will be better.' Describe the officer's return home and his joy at the recovery of his servant.

More things to do

Make get-well cards for someone who is ill. Use felt pens to decorate them or glue on coloured paper shapes. Together make up a short prayer to remind them about Jesus and write it in the cards.

Sharing with adults

Use the prayer in your cards to lead prayers for those who are ill.

Worship

Bible reading:
Matthew 8.5-9, 13. Jesus heals the officer's servant

Prayer:
Dear Jesus we trust you to care for all who are ill, especially ... May they remember that you are looking after them. Help us to remember that you care for us and to trust in you.

Song:
Praise him (JP:202) adding an extra verse 'Trust him'

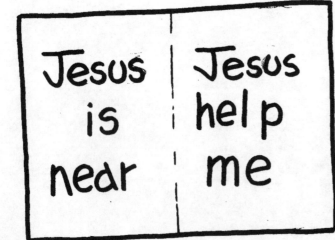

Take it home

Trusting Jesus

Draw pictures of people you trust to help you.

At home

At school

At Church

O God we know that you love us and care for us. Help us to trust you.

Matthew 8
5 to 9 and 13

Looking at Jesus

18 Jesus helps us to be brave

A Game

The children sit in a circle. When the leader says, 'the sea is rough' they stand up and 'bounce'; 'sea very rough' they jump; 'sea roars' they turn round on the spot and sit down; 'sea calm' remain seated. Call out the commands at random and see who is quickest at responding.

You will need
- ✔ boxes, egg boxes, sellotape, silver foil, pipe cleaners, yoghurt pots
- ✔ sheets of paper, felt pens, stapler

Story of stilling the storm

Tell the story of Jesus stilling the storm (Mark 4.35-40). The words in the gospel account are very vivid as they stand, although you will need to emphasise the peace and calm as Jesus and the disciples leave the crowds behind on the lakeside, the huge size of the lake (almost like being on the sea), the fear and panic of the disciples as the storm blows up. Finish with words like, 'The disciples were amazed at what had happened. They didn't understand it, but they knew that they were safe with Jesus, and did not need to be afraid of things like storms when he was with them.'

Talk and Do

Encourage the children to use their own ideas and to make junk models of imaginary monsters. Talk about the monsters, the noises they might make, what they do, how frightening they are. What makes the children afraid? What do they do about it? Who helps them to feel brave and safe?

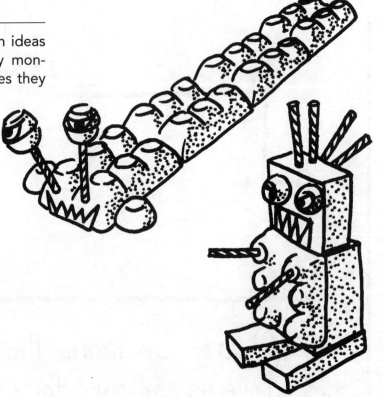

56

More things to do

Think of people who have done brave things e.g. children who have coped with illness or injuries, those who have rescued others from the water or from burning buildings. Use examples from recent news stories and from the children's own ideas. Make a simple book, each child writing about or drawing a picture of one story, and stapling them all together with a cover. Write a title for the book on the front and a simple prayer of thanks at the end.

Worship

Bible reading:
Mark 4.35-40 Jesus calms the storm

Prayer:
Jesus, when we are frightened please help us to know that you are always near to comfort us.

Song:
My God is so big (JP:169)

Sharing with adults

Show them the book of brave people, and say the prayer with them.

Take it home

Jesus helps us be brave

Colour this picture. Make the waves high and show the storm.

Jesus said "Be still." Draw the boat now it is calm

O God when things are difficult or frightening, help us to remember to ask for your help so that we can be brave.

Mark 4 35 to 40

Looking at Jesus

19 Being quiet with Jesus

A Game

One child stands at one end of the room facing the wall, the rest try to creep up to her from the other end of the room. The first child can turn round as often as she likes, and points to anyone who is seen to move. The first person to reach her taps her on the shoulder, and then takes her place as the game begins again.

Talk and Do

Give each child a piece of paper and a set of paper shapes. Ask them to work quietly while making the shapes into pictures. Look at each one in turn and talk about them quietly. Talk about times when we like to make a noise and times when we like to be quiet. When are we especially quiet in church and in our group?

You will need

- ✔ paper, a set of shapes made from gummed paper for each child,
- ✔ tablecloth, flowers, vase, candles, pictures of Jesus, a cross,
- ✔ quiet taped music

Story of Martha and Mary

Tell the story of Martha and Mary (Luke 10.38-42). Enlist the help of the children in thinking of all the things that Martha would want to do to get ready for Jesus and make him feel welcome. Contrast this with Mary who was anxious to give Jesus all her attention, and listen to him. Tell of Martha's crossness and her request to Jesus, 'Don't you care that my sister has left me to do all the work by myself? Tell her to come and help me!' Jesus replied, 'Martha, Martha! You are worried and troubled over so many things, but just one thing is needed, to listen to what I say, and that is what Mary is doing.' Ask the children what they think Martha did then. Let them mime the story.

More things to do

Set a table, with the children's help, so that it reminds them about Jesus. Use a cross, flowers, picture(s), a candle, as the children feel will be helpful. Sit quietly and listen to some music if possible, and then read a familiar story quietly to them. Jesus blessing the children would be suitable (Mark 10.13-16). Afterwards suggest that they close their eyes and think about the story. 'Can you see Jesus ... and the disciples ... and the children being called by Jesus ... How are they feeling now as Jesus holds them and blesses them?' Let them open their eyes and talk about the children whom Jesus had blessed telling their friends about it afterwards.

Worship

Bible reading:
Luke 10.38-42 Jesus visits Martha and Mary

Prayer:
Jesus, we know that you are alive and close to us now, although we cannot see you. Help us to be still and to think about you. Jesus, we love you and we want to know and love you more and more.

Song:
Be still and know (JP:22)

Sharing with adults

Read the Martha and Mary story while the children mime it for the congregation.

Looking at Jesus

20 Jesus is special

A Game

Think about the jobs which the children's parents do, and other jobs which adults do. Let the children take turns to mime the jobs which they would like to do when they grow up, so that the rest can guess them.

Talk and Do

Let each child decorate a crown. When they have finished, glue or staple the ends so that they fit the children's heads. Talk about people who wear crowns, kings and queens. What do they do? Think of other people who are important, or special to the children. Why do they think so?

You will need
- ✔ card shapes for crowns, shiny paper, sequins, braid, scissors, glue
- ✔ paper, felt pens

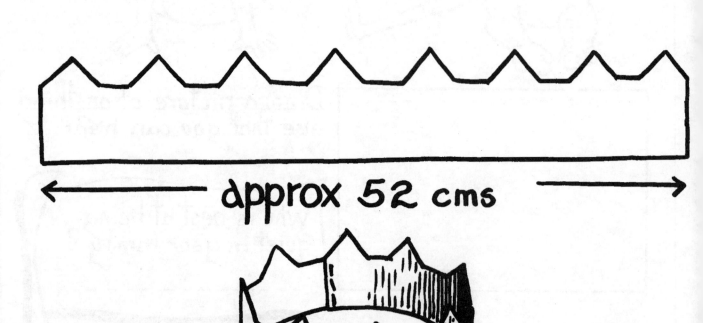

approx 52 cms

Story of Jesus the King

Develop a story along these lines: We have been thinking about lots of different jobs that you could do when you grow up. I expect that when Jesus was young he sometimes thought 'When I grow up I shall be a carpenter.' But sometimes he probably thought, 'When I grow up I shall tell people about God, my father, and help them to love him.' Joseph would have taught him how to work with wood so that he could help in the carpenter's shop. But Jesus must also have spent lots of time thinking about God, learning about him, and praying to him, so that he would be ready to do the work which God specially wanted him to do.

One day he went to the river Jordan where his cousin John was telling people to get ready for the coming of a special person whom God was sending to show them how to love him. When John saw Jesus he knew that he was that special person, and he baptised Jesus in the river. Jesus went away into a quiet place to think how he would do this special work. 'If I give food to everyone they will all crowd to see me,' he thought. 'But they will not really listen to me, only look for food. If I do something amazing like jumping off a high building and landing safely, they will all crowd to see me, but they will not really listen to me, only wait for the next amazing thing to happen. If I become a great ruler they will have to do what I say, but that will not help them to love God. I must find ways to show them what God's love is like.'

He found some men to help him, like Matthew and Peter and Andrew and James and John, and they went with him as he journeyed around telling stories to people, stories like the sower. He helped people who were in trouble and healed people like the Roman officer's servant. So those folk who listened to him and saw what he did began to see what God's love was like, and how God wanted them to behave. His closest friends, the disciples, realised that he was the special person whom God was sending to bring people back to loving him.

More things to do

Give each child a piece of paper, folded in two. On one half ask them to draw a picture about Jesus, and on the other half to draw themselves doing something helpful or loving for someone else. Write under the pictures. Jesus is special. I am special.

Worship

Bible reading:
Mark 1.9-11 Jesus is baptised

Prayer:
Jesus, we praise you. Jesus, we love you. Jesus, we thank you. Jesus, we know that you came to earth to help us all to love God. Help us to listen to stories about you, to pray to you, and to try to be loving to other people.

Song:
Alleluia, alleluia (JP:3)

Sharing with adults

Let the children wear their crowns, and let each show their pictures to an adult of their choice.

Take it home

Jesus is special

Help the King to find his crown

Ask your family who their special people are _____
_____

Jesus is our King.
Jesus loves us.
We praise and thank him for all that he does for us and for everyone.

Mark 1
9 to 11